EXPLORE COLONIAL AMERICA

COLONIAL JAMESTOWN

Sarah Gilman

Enslow Publishing
101 W. 23rd Street
Suite 240
New York, NY 10011
USA
enslow.com

Published in 2017 by Enslow Publishing, LLC.
101 W. 23rd Street, Suite 240, New York, NY 10011

Library of Congress Cataloging-in-Publication Data
Names: Gilman, Sarah.
Title: Colonial Jamestown / Sarah Gilman.
Description: New York, NY : Enslow Publishing, 2017. | Series: Explore Colonial America | Includes bibliographical references and index. | Audience: Grades 4-6. | Audience: Ages 9+
Identifiers: LCCN 2015050572| ISBN 9780766078710 (library bound) | ISBN 9780766078772 (pbk.) | ISBN 9780766078598 (6-pack)
Subjects: LCSH: Jamestown (Va.)--History--17th century--Juvenile literature.| Jamestown (Va.)--Biography--Juvenile literature. | Virginia--History--Colonial period, ca. 1600-1775--Juvenile literature.
Classification: LCC F234.J3 G54 2017 | DDC 975.5/4251--dc23
LC record available at http://lccn.loc.gov/2015050572

To Our Readers: We have done our best to make sure all website addresses in this book were active and appropriate when we went to press. However, the author and the publisher have no control over and assume no liability for the material available on those websites or on any web sites they may link to. Any comments or suggestions can be sent by e-mail to customerservice@enslow.com.

Portions of this book originally appeared in the book *Explore Colonial Jamestown with Elaine Landau* by Elaine Landau.

Photo Credits: Throughout book: javarman/Shutterstock.com (tan background), STILLFX/Shutterstock.com (American flag background), Peliken/Shutterstock.com (white stars on blue background); cover, p. 1 Zack Frank/Shutterstock.com; p. 4 Public domain/File:Jamestown Island (1958 base map).png/Wikimedia Commons; pp. 6, 15, 26, 30 © North Wind Picture Archives; p. 7 Print Collector/Getty Images; pp. 10, 18 Joseph Sohm/Shutterstock.com; pp. 11, 19, 29, 38 MPI/Getty Images; pp. 14, 33 Hulton Archive/Getty Images; p. 21 Kean Collection/Getty Images; p. 23 Library of Congress; p. 35 Kean Collection/Getty Images; p. 36 The massacre of the settlers in 1622, plate VII, from 'America, Part XIII', German edition, 1628 (coloured engraving), Merian, Matthaus, the Elder (1593-1650) / Virginia Historical Society, Richmond, Virginia, USA / Bridgeman Images; p. 39 Mladen Antonov/Getty Images; p. 40 Mannie Garcia/Getty Images; p. 43 Public domain/File:Pocahontas at the court of King James.png/Wikimedia Commons.

CONTENTS

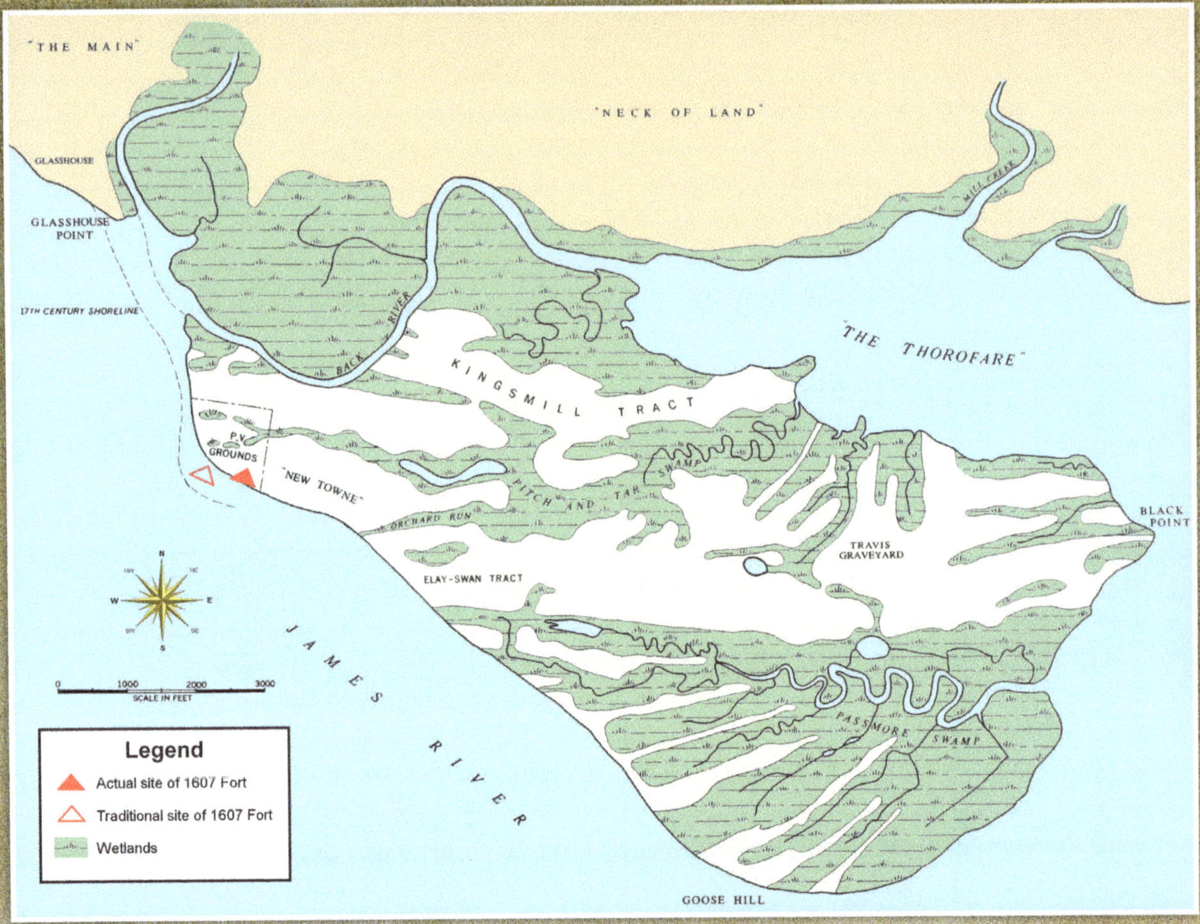

On the banks of the James River, the settlers funded by the Virginia Company built Jamestown Colony, the first permanent English settlement in North America.

CHAPTER ONE

THE NEW WORLD

In the early seventeenth century, North America was still a mystery to most Europeans. They had heard exciting tales about this wild, new world. Explorers described it as a rich paradise. However, few Europeans had traveled there.

Some English settlers had gone to North America in the late 1500s. Twice they tried to start a settlement on Roanoke Island. This is an island in the area we know today as North Carolina. (Back then, it was part of Virginia.) Both attempts failed. So, in 1600 there were still no English settlements in North America.

REASONS TO SETTLE

People in England knew of the failed settlements. Yet, some still longed to cross the Atlantic. They wanted to go for different reasons.

Europeans were aware of the challenges involved in settling in America. In the sixteenth century, Roanoke became known as the "lost colony" because its residents mysteriously vanished.

Religion was an important reason to go. The Church of England wanted to bring the Christian religion to the American Indians.

Great Britain's King James I also wanted glory. Britain's rivals—France and Spain—had settlements in North America. Britain's king wanted his share of this land.

The hope of discovering great riches drew many others to the New World. Some dreamed of finding gold and jewels.

King James I was in a competition with France and Spain to colonize North America. The settlement of Jamestown would be the first step of the colonization of the Americas for England. Its peak was reached in the eighteenth century.

Still others sought a quicker route to Asia for jewels, silks, and spices. Spices add flavor to food. They also help to keep meat fresh. Was there a shorter way to reach Asia from Britain? Some hoped to find a sea route through North America.

EXPLORE THE FACTS

VALUABLE SPICES

Spices were worth much more money in 1607 than they are today. This is because spices came from Asia and Indonesia. This was a part of the world that was once very hard for people to get to.

The Virginia Company of London dreamed of building a thriving colony in North America. There was money to be made across the sea. The company had received permission from King James I to start a settlement. By December 1606, the company was set to do exactly that. They had found a group of people that were ready to brave the Atlantic Ocean and three sturdy ships to take them to what was then called the New World.

CHAPTER TWO

JAMESTOWN ISLAND

The Virginia Company sent 144 people from England. Of the group, 104 were settlers and the rest were crew—all men.

A LONG VOYAGE

The group left on December 20, 1606, in three ships. These were the *Discovery*, the *Godspeed*, and the *Susan Constant*. Captain Christopher Newport was in charge of the voyage.

The difficult trip across the Atlantic took about four months. There were storms at sea. Much of the food rotted. Some of the passengers became ill. Also, the ships made stops at a few islands in the Caribbean Sea. This was far south from where they were supposed to land in Virginia. They were glad to finally reach land at 4 a.m. on April 26, 1607. Yet it took another two weeks to pick a site for the colony.

The Virginia Company sent three ships carrying cargo and passengers to the New World. *Discovery*, *Godspeed*, and *Susan Constant* set out for North America in December 1606.

EXPLORE THE FACTS

A LONG JOURNEY

The settlers didn't know what to expect when they landed. Since their journey took four months, they had a lot of time to think about it! Today, a journey from England to Virginia would take about eight hours by plane.

A GOOD SPOT

On May 14, they settled on a place they named Jamestown Island. It was on the James River, about sixty miles from the mouth of Chesapeake Bay. This was in the region we now call Virginia. Jamestown Island was not really an island, but was actually a peninsula. That is a section of land surrounded by water on three

The colonists finally landed at Cape Henry on the Chesapeake Bay. After traveling up the James River, they chose a site on Jamestown Island, which turned out to be problematic.

sides. Only a very thin strip of land connected it to the rest of Virginia.

Captain Newport and the others liked the spot. The water around the peninsula was deep. Their ships could be brought near the shore. That made loading and unloading vessels easier.

The new land also offered some protection from Indian attacks. It was almost completely surrounded by water. That made it much easier to defend.

The colony would be safe from Britain's enemies as well. Jamestown was near the Atlantic Ocean. Lookouts could be posted to spot approaching ships from Spain or other countries unfriendly toward Britain.

The settlers thought they had made a good choice. Unfortunately, they would soon find out that they had not. There were some things they had not considered. Hard times were ahead for this adventurous group of English colonists.

CHAPTER THREE

TROUBLE BEGINS

The settlers soon learned that Jamestown Island was not a good spot. The peninsula had many marshy areas that were filled with stale, dirty water. As a result, there were a lot of mosquitoes. The mosquitoes carried disease. Frequent flooding on the peninsula made things worse.

The settlers had no clean drinking water. The James River's water was brackish (salty). It was not fit to drink. The more the settlers drank it, the thirstier they became. It even made the people sick.

THE NEED FOR LEADERS

There were other problems, too. More than half of the settlers were British "gentlemen" who were not used to hard work. They were only interested in getting rich by finding gold or by trading things they found to Britain. The other settlers were mostly skilled craftsmen. They could make tools, weapons, jewelry, and other useful items. Only a few men had farming skills.

After they finally chose a site on which to build their settlement, the colony's men began chopping trees for wood to use in the construction of homes and a fortress.

There was also no strong leader at Jamestown. The Virginia Company had picked a group of men to form a government. Among those chosen to serve on the governing council was John Smith. During the voyage, he had been disrespectful to the English gentlemen. Captain Newport even charged him with rebellion and some wanted to hang him. Now he was to be one of their leaders. One of the reasons he was picked was that he had experience as a leader. Before the voyage, Smith had led other soldiers as a captain in the army.

INDIAN ATTACK

Life at Jamestown was not easy. Right away, more than two hundred Paspahegh Indians attacked the settlement. The settlers were unprepared. They had not even finished building their fort.

The settlers quickly ran to one of their ships for protection. They fired their muskets and cannons from there. These were weapons that the American Indians did not have. Even if the

The colonists soon found their settlement under attack from local American Indians. Although their fort was still under construction, they were able to seek shelter in their ships.

settlers did not hit their attackers, the sound of the guns often scared the Indians away. Nevertheless, one settler was killed. Eleven others were wounded.

This marked the start of a troubled time between the settlers and the different groups of American Indians that lived in the area. Sometimes there would be peace and friendship. Other years were filled with war and much bloodshed.

CHAPTER FOUR

DEATH COMES TO JAMESTOWN

Things continued to decline for the settlers. The summer of 1607 was terrible. A large number of the settlers became deathly ill.

DISEASE AND HUNGER

Some settlers had malaria, a serious disease spread by mosquitoes. Others suffered from typhoid. This is an illness caused by germs in food and water. Many settlers got sick drinking impure river water.

Not many crops had been planted and the supply ships from England were late. The settlers were weak and hungry.

During the summer, death became common at Jamestown. Often, several settlers died on the same day. At times, those who lived barely had the strength to bury the dead.

The fall brought cooler weather. Yet by then, more than half of the original settlers were dead.

A HERO EMERGES

Jamestown badly needed good leaders. But most on the governing council were not up to the task. The real hero at Jamestown proved to be John Smith.

Smith began trading with the Paspaheghs. The Paspaheghs gave the settlers bread and corn. In return, the settlers gave the Paspaheghs trinkets and other items.

With food in their stomachs, the settlers felt better. However, there were fewer of them now. Even the English gentlemen had to work.

Smith made everyone farm. They also had to finish the buildings they had started. Life was better at Jamestown, but not for long.

Half of the original settlers died by the end of the summer of 1607. Disease in the form of typhoid and malaria got to many, and malnutrition and hunger to others.

The Jamestown settlers invited the Paspaheghs inside their fort, where they engaged in trade. The colonists obtained much needed food in exchange for trinkets.

EXPLORE THE FACTS

CORN SAVES THE DAY

The American Indians had enough corn to trade with the Jamestown settlers. Corn could be dried and ground into corn meal. The corn meal could then be used to make bread.

CHAPTER FIVE

JOHN SMITH GETS INTO TROUBLE

The settlers had an enemy. His name was Powhatan. Powhatan was a powerful Indian leader in charge of more than thirty groups or tribes. Powhatan's group were named the Powhatan Indians, after him. Powhatan did not like the settlers. He saw them as invaders.

TAKEN CAPTIVE

In December 1607, John Smith left Jamestown with a small group of men. He wanted to explore the surrounding region, or area. While away, the group was attacked by Powhatan Indians. Some of Smith's men were killed, but Smith was taken captive.

Powhatan was a powerful leader who organized and led thirty different American Indian tributaries. Powhatan did not trust the Jamestown settlers.

Smith was brought before the great chief Powhatan. He enjoyed a feast with the American Indians. Then two stones were brought out. They were placed in front of Powhatan.

At that point, things did not look good for Smith. He was dragged over to the stones and thrown on the ground. The Indians placed Smith's head on the stones. They stood above Smith with raised clubs. John Smith was sure that he was going to die. He thought that the Indians were about to crush his skull.

POCAHONTAS TO THE RESCUE

Just at that moment, an Indian girl named Pocahontas came running out. She was only about twelve years old. Pocahontas was Powhatan's favorite daughter. She begged her father to stop his men. But the chief would not listen.

So Pocahontas raced over to Smith and put her head on his. If John Smith died, she would, too. Powhatan told his men to put their clubs down. Pocahontas had saved John Smith's life.

The story John Smith told of his first meeting with Powhatan is famous. However, we do not know if it is true. Smith often told stories that made him look brave or important.

Pocahontas probably did meet John Smith that evening. But what she really did that night is not clear. Some people think that Pocahontas did not act on her own. They believe that her father told her to save Smith.

Powhatan was a very wise chief. He may have known that killing a Jamestown leader was a bad idea. Perhaps he wanted John Smith to owe him a favor.

Legend states that Powhatan's people were seconds away from killing Captain John Smith, when Pocahontas stepped in to rescue the colonist.

A SECOND NEAR DEATH

Smith returned to Jamestown. A few days later, Pocahontas brought food to the colony. By then, the harsh winter of 1608 had set in. The settlers were grateful for her help.

They were less pleased with John Smith. Many of the gentlemen were angry at having to work. Others blamed Smith for the deaths of the men he went exploring with. The governing council sentenced John Smith to hang.

Yet, John Smith's life was spared again. This time Captain Newport rescued him. On January 4, 1608, Newport returned to the colony from England. He brought supplies and more settlers. Newport had Smith released. He knew that Smith got along well with the American Indians. The captain felt that the colony needed Smith alive.

It was a good decision. On January 7, 1608, a terrible fire swept through Jamestown. It destroyed the settlers' homes, food, and supplies. After the fire, the Indians brought them more food.

By spring, the colony had been rebuilt. Captain Newport again left for England. The settlers planted new crops and hoped for much better times.

EXPLORE THE FACTS

NEWPORT NEWS

Captain Newport left his mark on the area. The settlement of Newport News—now Newport News, Virginia—was named after him.

CHAPTER SIX

A STRUGGLING COLONY

After months of getting the colony back on track, John Smith became president of the governing council in September 1608. He divided the men into work crews. The crews fished, farmed, and chopped down trees for lumber. Some lumber was used for buildings in the colony. Lumber was also sent back to England to be sold there.

In October, Captain Newport brought more settlers. Among them were the colony's first women. John Smith put them to work, too. Smith also made the men train with weapons. Dealings with the Indians had become less friendly. Smith expected more trouble.

The Jamestown colonists tried to turn a profit for the Virginia Company by exporting lumber back to Europe. Unfortunately, this was not enough.

EXPLORE THE FACTS

THE SETTLEMENT

The buildings of the Jamestown settlement were inside a fort. The houses were small but kept the colonists safe from bad weather. A long, wooden wall called a palisade surrounded the fort.

CHANGES IN THE COLONY

The settlement did well under Smith's leadership. Yet, the colony still had not begun to earn a profit. So the Virginia Company made some changes. It did away with the governing council. Instead, a governor would be put in charge.

John Smith also had a bad accident. A sack of gunpowder exploded, badly injuring him. He returned to England in the summer of 1609. The settlement would not be the same without John Smith.

CHAPTER SEVEN

NEW LEADERSHIP

John Smith's departure was not good for the colony. The new governor still had not arrived, so there was no leader. People did not work as hard as they should have.

Things grew worse between the settlers and the American Indians. Powhatan no longer traded with the settlers. Now fear replaced friendship. Any settler who left the fort was attacked. The men were afraid to fish or hunt. They felt like prisoners in their own colony.

THE STARVING TIME

This led to the worst months in Jamestown's history. The winter of 1609 to 1610 was known as "the starving time." Settlers had almost nothing to eat. They killed and ate their horses. They even ate the rats they caught.

The winter that began in 1609 was known as “the starving time” for the Jamestown settlers. With no food and no hope of trading with their Native American neighbors, all but sixty colonists died.

Lord De La Warr arrived in 1610 to help turn the colony around. He was appointed governor of Virginia, but it is a different U.S. state that is named after him: Delaware.

People died of starvation and disease daily. Some used their last bit of strength to dig their own graves. There had been about five hundred Jamestown settlers before that winter. Only about sixty were left by the spring of 1610.

Several ships carrying new settlers arrived in May 1610. The newcomers were shocked at what they found. The survivors looked like walking skeletons. Little was left of the colony as well. The remaining settlers had taken apart most of the buildings. They used the lumber for firewood. It was all they had to keep warm during the winter. The survivors were anxious to leave Jamestown. The new arrivals wanted to leave, too. They saw that there was no food.

HELP IS ON THE WAY

Yet as it turned out, none of them left. The very next morning, another ship arrived with food and supplies. A man named Lord De La Warr was on it. He was the colony's new governor. Like John Smith, De La Warr quickly took charge. People planted crops and rebuilt houses. Nevertheless, De La Warr left the colony in March 1611 because of poor health. He had not lasted a year at Jamestown.

The next leader arrived in Jamestown on May 19, 1611. He was a former soldier named Sir Thomas Dale. The Virginia Company wanted Dale to find a better site for the settlement. Dale chose a spot upriver that was not as marshy as Jamestown. Today it is known as Curles Neck. Back then, it was called Henrico.

American Indians were already living in that area. That did not matter to Dale. He fought the Indians and took their land. Dale saw this as Britain's right. The Indians saw things differently. This would lead to problems later.

CHAPTER EIGHT

GROWING PROBLEMS

Some settlers remained at Jamestown. One named John Rolfe began planting tobacco there. At the same time, the Henrico settlement grew. Other Virginia settlements were started as well.

POCAHONTAS IS KIDNAPPED

In time, more settlers came to Virginia. Before long, they outnumbered the American Indians there. At times, the settlers killed the Indians to get their land and corn.

British settlers also stole young Indian children. They wanted their captives to become Christians. In 1613, Pocahontas was among those kidnapped. She was about sixteen years old at the time.

The settlers had been anxious to get Powhatan's daughter. They expected him to give them corn and other things to get her back. At first, Powhatan agreed to the settlers' demands. However,

Tobacco turned out to be a winning crop for the Virginia soil. Once the colonists began farming tobacco, the colony became much more profitable.

EXPLORE THE FACTS

LADY REBECCA

When Pocahontas converted to Christianity she took the name Lady Rebecca. Her marriage to John Rolfe brought peace between the Powhatan and the English colonists.

the colonists never received what they wanted. Meanwhile, Pocahontas became a Christian. On April 5, 1614, she also married one of the settlers—the tobacco grower John Rolfe.

THE HOUSE OF BURGESSES

As time passed, Jamestown had different leaders. The Virginia Company picked the governors. But all this changed in July 1619. At that point, the colonists got to pick their own leaders. This new group of leaders was known as the House of Burgesses. Twenty-two men were elected to represent the settlers. The House of Burgesses was the first elected government in North America. It passed many different laws. Some laws were about proper behavior. Others had to do with the American Indians. Still other laws involved deciding how much people should pay for tobacco.

Between 1619 and 1622, Jamestown grew. More women arrived. Soon, there were families at Jamestown. Many people began growing tobacco. More land was needed for this. So the settlers spread out. They started large tobacco growing farms called plantations. Numerous tobacco growers did quite well. Yet their lives were not problem-free. Before long there was more trouble with the American Indians.

OPECHANCANOUGH

Powhatan had died in 1618. Another strong leader had taken over. His name was Opechancanough. Opechancanough did not like the English either. They had taken too much land and treated his people badly.

The settlers kidnapped Powhatan's daughter, Pocahontas, and held her for ransom. While in captivity, Pocahontas converted to Christianity and married colonist John Rolfe.

On March 22, 1622, Opechancanough struck back. He and his men staged an early morning attack. The settlers were caught off guard. Some were killed at the breakfast table. Others were struck down while working in the fields. Opechancanough's men killed 347 settlers. That was about one-third of the colony. The Indians also burned the settlers' homes, plantations, and ironworks.

By now, the Virginia Company had grown weary. Jamestown was always plagued by problems. King James I was disappointed, too. He took away the company's charter, which was the agreement the colony had with the Virginia Company. Jamestown simply became a British colony. The Virginia Company no longer had a claim to it.

In what became known as the Indian Massacre of 1622, Opechancanough and his men attacked Jamestown and other communities along the James River.

CHAPTER NINE

THE END OF JAMESTOWN

By the 1640s, many craftsmen and merchants had shops in Jamestown. The colony had glassblowers, carpenters, jewelry makers, weavers, and winemakers. Some of the richer families had large two-story brick homes.

There were also more tobacco plantations nearby. Settlers no longer feared starving. Enough food was grown each year. The bad times seemed to be over.

ANOTHER ATTACK

However, in April 1644, Opechancanough struck again. It was another surprise attack. This time about five hundred settlers were killed. Some escaped to nearby forts that had been built. Many refused to return to their homes for months. They were afraid of another attack.

After years of building and rebuilding the settlement, surviving disease and starvation, and enduring American Indian attacks, the people of Jamestown abandoned the colony.

The trouble between the American Indians and the settlers continued. At times, the settlers disagreed on how to deal with the native people. This led to fighting among themselves.

CLOSING TIME

All the fighting weakened Jamestown. Many people moved to a nearby settlement, Middle Plantation. The area would later be called Williamsburg.

By the late 1690s, few people lived in Jamestown anymore. It was no longer a center for trade or business. In 1698, much of what was left of the settlement was destroyed in a fire. Yet that small struggling colony has not been forgotten. Jamestown has a special place in our nation's history.

JAMESTOWN TODAY

The original Jamestown settlement is gone. However, the colony has been rebuilt and serves as an education center. It now looks much like it did three hundred years ago. Visitors can see the fort, houses, craft shops, and even a rebuilt American Indian village. Tour guides dress as the early settlers did. They teach visitors about the colony's history.

The area where the Jamestown settlement once stood is now an archaeological site. Researchers have unearthed artifacts, such as this copper medallion in the likeness of Powhatan.

Today, visitors can tour Jamestown Settlement, a living history museum not far from the original site of the settlement. The park features replicas of the three ships used to sail to Virginia, a reconstruction of the fort, and an example of a Powhatan village.

Archeologists at Jamestown have uncovered items the colonists used. Archeologists are people who dig up old objects to study the past. This has helped us know even more about the settlers' exciting lives.

EXPLORE THE FACTS

THE NEXT CENTURIES

Jamestown Island was used during the American Revolution. American and British soldiers were exchanged at the military post there. Confederate soldiers also stayed there during the Civil War.

CHAPTER TEN

FOLLOWING UP ON

Many of the people involved with the Jamestown settlement went on to live interesting lives. Here is information on a few of them.

JOHN SMITH

After his injury in 1609, John Smith never returned to Virginia. He made another trip to North America in 1614 to explore New England. Before his death in 1621, John Smith wrote a number of books. Some told of his adventures in Jamestown.

POCAHONTAS

Pocahontas and her husband, John Rolfe, and son visited Britain in 1616. While there, Pocahontas met the king and queen. Pocahontas's visit made people more aware of the Jamestown colony. In March 1617, Pocahontas and her family boarded a ship to return to Virginia. However, Pocahontas soon became

Pocahontas and John Rolfe were presented to King James I. The American Indian was presented to British society to promote investment opportunities in the Jamestown colony.

very ill. She was taken ashore to Gravesend, England. She died there on March 21, 1617.

OPECHANCANOUGH

Following the 1644 uprising, Opechancanough was captured. He had been caught once before but escaped. This time he was not as lucky. While imprisoned at Jamestown, he was murdered. Some say that a prison guard killed him. After his death, the Powhatan Indians were forced to sign a peace treaty. It gave the settlers even more of the Indians' land.

TIMELINE

1607—The Virginia Company settlers arrive at Jamestown Island on May 14.

1608—A terrible fire sweeps through the colony on January 7. In September, John Smith becomes president of the governing council.

1609—John Smith is wounded that summer when a sack of gunpowder explodes. He goes back to England.

1609–1610—The winter months were known as the "starving time." Many Jamestown settlers died from lack of food.

1610—Lord De La Warr arrives in Jamestown in May and leaves in March 1611.

1613—Pocahontas is kidnapped by the English settlers.

1618—Powhatan dies.

1619—Jamestown's House of Burgesses is started in July.

1622—Opechancanough attacks, killing 347 settlers.

1644—Opechancanough launches a second major attack. This time 500 settlers are killed.

1698—Jamestown is destroyed in a fire.

1994—Archeological digs begin at Jamestown to recover items from the colony.

GLOSSARY

ARCHEOLOGIST—Someone who learns about the past by digging up and studying old buildings and objects.

CAPTIVE—A prisoner.

CHARTER—An agreement and/or document.

ELECTED—Chosen to be a leader by the people one will represent.

GOVERNING COUNCIL—A government used by the early Jamestown settlers. The leaders of the governing council were picked by the Virginia Company, not elected by the colonists.

INVADERS—People who fight to take over another country.

JOURNEY—A long trip.

PALISADE—A fence made from wooden or iron spikes that encloses an area.

PENINSULA—An area of land surrounded by water on three sides.

PLANTATION—A large farm.

PROFIT—Money gained.

TREATY—An agreement of peace reached between two parties.

TRINKETS—Small items that some people find valuable.

FURTHER READING

Benoit, Peter. *The Jamestown Colony.* New York: Children's Press, 2012.

Downey, Fran and Lana Constantini. *Jamestown.* Monterey, CA: National Geographic, 2013.

Higgins, Melissa. *The Jamestown Colony.* Minneapolis: ABDO Publishing Company, 2013.

Levy, Janey. *Life in Jamestown Colony.* New York: Gareth Stevens Publishing, 2014.

Ransom, Candice F. *Why Did English Settlers Come to Virginia? And Other Questions About the Jamestown Settlement.* Minneapolis: Lerner Publications, 2011.

FOR MORE INFORMATION

JAMESTOWN REDISCOVERY

www.historicjamestowne.org/history/history-of-jamestown/

Visit the site of the archeological project at Jamestown. See pictures of the interesting items found and learn about the latest discoveries.

VIRTUAL JAMESTOWN

www.virtualjamestown.org

This is a wonderful online history site about the Jamestown settlement. Do not miss the map section for a great view of original maps of Virginia.

WELCOME TO JAMESTOWN

www.ab.mec.edu/jamestown/jamestown.html

This site provides a detailed overview of what life was like for early Jamestown settlers. There is lots of information on village life, celebrations, and survival.

INDEX